# MENTAL HEALTH AND ME

## R WOOD

Life in Words Poetry

## About the Author

Rick Wood is a British writer born in Cheltenham.

His love for writing came at an early age, as did his battle with mental health. After defeating his demons, he grew up and became a stand-up comedian, then a drama and English teacher, before giving it all up to become a full-time author.

He now lives in Loughborough, where he makes his living from writing horror - and, more recently, poetry.

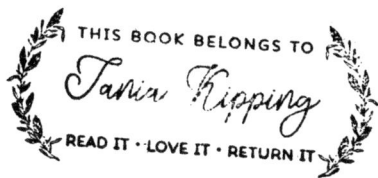

THIS BOOK BELONGS TO
*Janis Kipping*
READ IT · LOVE IT · RETURN IT

# Introduction

Welcome to my second poetry anthology!

I decided that, in my follow up to Life in Words, I needed a theme...

And that theme wasn't tough to come up with at all.

In my time on this earth, I have suffered from OCD, bipolar disorder and Tourette's Syndrome, among other things.

I have faced therapy and medication, and finally got my life on track.

However, following the breakup of a long relationship, I had to let go of the life I'd created for myself after conquering my issues.

Friends I had were through this relationship, my house was a joint mortgage, my mental health was at its all-time best - I'd built something great.

I left this life and went back to my parent's at the age of 31.

I was, inevitably, low. And I came the closest I've come to returning to the lows I used to drown in.

The darkness ended, of course. Me and my puppy found a house. I learnt to be happy on my own. And I let myself fall for someone else.

During that time of darkness, I turned to words. I spent my evenings articulating how I felt in the only way I could.

Through poetry.

This book is the collection of that poetry.

Everything I felt is in this book.

After the poems you will find an afterword where I go through each poem and explain its background.

I believe that poetry should mean something different to each person that reads it - but, if you would like an insight into how the poems were put together, please have a read.

I hope you enjoy the collection of poems, and I hope you find some that you can relate to. Through this, I hope it makes your struggles just that little bit better.

Rick

# The Struggle

Please,
Give me a medal
For getting out of bed.

It was warm in there
And the world is getting colder.

The movement
A rotation
A swivel
The swing of the legs
Tufts of carpet through toes
And a slight push
Of my arms
And I'm out.

I can see it.

I know what to do.

I can envision the process.

But somehow
I am still here.

# Pointless Death

I don't think I can get
Any lower than this.

It seems like writing you these words
In meaningless syntax
As if there's a point to a metaphor
Is the thing
The only thing
Between me and the noose
Or setting this raging fire
To this house.

These aren't words for critical acclaim
Or rhyme or deeper meaning
Some teacher would attach
If these words had enough craft
To be taught.

They are a vacant expression
Of complicated composition that

Truly, truly means
Little but diatribe
About a misery
Not at all unique
To every stanza already written.

I write these words
Because they are harder
Than a blade
But leave less scars.

Oh, look, another verse
And a new line
Enjambment to symbolise the ongoing nature of pain
It's the same
And I blame
Everyone else until I blame myself
Then blame no one.

Nothing is ever at fault.
People just are.

Walking around life doesn't get you far
But I'd sooner end it all
Right now than just
Keep rambling to a page
Who will never hold me back
And will be destroyed by water
Which means
It cannot even survive my cry.

But I can die.

Oh, I can die

And go down in glory I'll never get
So my obituary can be
The wrapping for
Tomorrow's fish and chips.

See, I have a purpose after all.

Give me a reason to save
Suicide for next week
Because it's looking bleak
There's nothing else on my todo list to do.

So goodbye I say with words
That mean even less
Than the life it took to type them
And even less
Than each syllable I just
Wasted my time
Writing.

# Say Okay to the World

I'll be okay.

That's what you want me to say,
Isn't it?

No more talking can be done
No more change is going to come
So it's okay
I'm fine
I'm okay.

Aren't I?

There's nothing you can do
There's nothing I can do
So I have to be okay
I have to be.

Surely?

Is that would I should say?

But what if I open up with honesty
And say things really bother me
That it burns and rages
At the imprisonment of my skin
With an anger I can't justify
And a despair I can't console
But it's old
I felt this way five months ago
So it's time for me to be better
So if you ask me I can't just go and say
There's no way
I can bear another five
Of this alive.
I thought my thoughts belonged to me
But they keep fighting with each other
And ridiculing my every move
With so many voices
Until I want a pit
To scream into
And keep screaming
Until my lungs combust and burst out into ash
And my throat is like a game of Kerplunk with razors
And the whole fucking world
Can hear this incessant agony.

...

...

...

...

But no.
It's cool, I'm back from the fall.

I'll be okay.

That's what I'm meant to say, after all.

# Endless Talking

I can still smell you on my hoody.
A scent that once made me miss you
Is a stench
That becomes a welcome pain.

I can still sense you behind me,
The pain in my back,
And I fumble in the darkness
For your arm
To pull it over or brush it off
But the kiss on my neck doesn't come
And I roll
Into the empty space
Where you
Used to reside.

The trial I put you on
Produced a split jury
And a judge
Too eager to condemn.

Maybe you should have stayed.
Maybe I should have left.

Or maybe we should have stopped the words.

They mean nothing, after all.

# Okay

I wanted to be that feeling you get
When you look at the stars
And feel so small
But know that it's okay.
That non-existential spark of light
Is just evidence
Not only of our insignificance
But that there is more;
More than just this;
More than mundane arguments
That never go one way or the other.
It is about deeper conversations
That never give solutions,
Only ask questions
For which there need not be answers.

I can't ever make a decision
But I'll be what you need to miss,
I just have this predisposition
To fall in love with every person I kiss,

And I wish
And I wish
And I wish...

Knowing that wishes are just words.
You can say what you want
To nothing but space.
Then, as the words are lost,
They are just as our lives are
When we are gone.

And somehow,
I think that that's okay.

# Fading

I can feel you fading from my body.
Against my better wishes
I find my sense of you
Disengaged
Running away and
I never even noticed.

I can feel you feeling neutral.
Excitement I once had
Is not replaced by hatred.
Just a void
No longer needed to be filled.

Where did it go?

Now we're in
For a conversation
More difficult than a
Faulty maths equation
That once upon a time

Made the stars implode.
They still implode only
The light doesn't reach us
For another 16,000 years.

I can feel you failing.
Our home is not a battlefield
It's just a house
With a for sale sign
Behind the picket fence.

They said it takes work.
But no one ever said how
To restore love.
You can work through anything
But how can you work
Through nothing?

I don't see a way out
Of a hole
I sit in with the light on.

Goodbye, I mean well.
We'll be going through hell
And it may be scary
But trust me –
It's only temporary.

# They Call it Rock Bottom

They call it rock bottom.
I call it the tip of the iceberg.
You call it all the clichés
Your clueless mouth can make
As if a tired old idiom
Can do anything with the poisoned water under the
     bridge
Or the thing that killed me and didn't make me
     stronger.

They call it rock bottom.
Then I lifted it up and saw
All these rocks underneath.
You swept the stones aside and told me to move on
But how can I move on
When I'm still falling beneath the rubble.

They call it rock bottom.
I call it tears my parents don't see.
Huffs I let out in solitude

And thoughts I disguise with a smile.

They call it rock bottom.
As if THEY have any idea
About the pain THEY talk over
As THEY give me what THEY can be bothered to give
In order to label me cured and move onto the
Next victim THEY have waiting outside.
Sorry, did I say victim?
I meant *patient*.

They call it rock bottom.
I call it Everest.
I look to the sky
And look among the stars
At everything that makes me insignificant
And I can see rock bottom
Above them all.

They call it rock bottom
And you say it too.
I resent you for the words
As if there's something else you can do.

# This Pill

They gave me this pill.
So light
But with such heavy expectation.

1cm
To fix my life.
1 a day
To keep the feelings inside.
Fill my prescription
And empty my mind.
And if this pill doesn't work
You can say that you tried.

Long name
Required symptoms
Track record
A slip of paper
All ticks the boxes needed
To make me numb.

They gave me this promise
That I take without water
For my blood to bus around.

Does this mean
I get to be normal?
Not to feel?
Not to need
A way out of life?

And what's this?
Side effects!
Glory, glory,
Halleluiah!
Tired all the time
And I don't want to fuck.

Tell the woman I love
That we're out of luck
That I thought I was fixed
But I was mistook
We solved the issue
This pill's all it took
But now my dick is numb
And my soul has been sucked.

They gave me this pill
And I think
I don't know what to say anymore.

# Inside

Sometimes
I run the hot tap
Until my hands are red
Just to see if I
Can still feel a pain
Outside of my skull.

I wait until the wincing
Replaces the smile
I painted upon my face.

And it feels good.

That I can finally feel something physically
That matches the rage inside my mind.

# Graffiti

It's marked in red pen
Amongst the shit
Upon the toilet door.
A profound quote
Engrained in it
But heaven knows what for.
If thoughts are profound
And you've something to say
To cast light upon us all.
Don't go on a march
Never protest
Just place it upon the toilet wall.

# Where Are You?

I write these words
Because I can't write you to life.
So I write your absence.
How can I miss
Someone I don't know exists
Is beyond me.

But I wait for you.
Oh, I wait, how I do.

Maybe, hopefully, someday
There will no longer
Be need
For these words.

# I'm Not Really Here

For six years I watched you disappear.
Now I could die in this empty room
And no one would know.
My dog would chew my bones
And maybe the news would reach you
In a month or so.

Would you come to my funeral
If I was the last person
You'd loved to life?

Because I loved you to death.

Now here I am.
Here you aren't.

It worked out just as planned.

# Why Did You Do That To Yourself?

I did it for the attention.

I did it because I was too stubborn to mention
In case it caused tension that I'm not okay.

I did it because I can
And you try but can't understand
Why I'd grab a weapon in my hand
And do this day by day.

I did it so I could show the inane
A visual representation of my pain
Not that they're to blame for my feeling this way
It just shows them physically what I can't find the words
    to say
And when they ask about this thing I choose
I'll just give them any excuse.

I did it because it's part of the farce
And I get a few sets of scars

And for four months this performance
Gives me a mark that lasts.

I did it because it's easier than not doing it.

I smashed the photo frame and ruined her face
And the broken glass waited in place
So why not?

It would have been a waste
To leave the broken edge to rot.

I did for every reason and none at all.

I did it. And you can't change that anymore.

And I know I'll do it again when life gets as it was
    before.

# My Parent's House

There's pictures of me on the wall
But none of them I'd choose.

I sit on a sofa with too many cushions
And slide down on a throw.

I no longer make the coffee.
It is made for me.

And I no longer use my key.

And I wonder
At what point I'd known
That this house I grew up in
Is no longer my home.

# Yawn

What is the point
Of these incessant words
Going around and around my notepad
With no solutions or comforts
Just words
Words words words and nothing more.

That's all I am.
That's all you are.

I should be more but syntax
Is my downfall.

Like scattered stars in the sky
All planets already imploded
But at least with more purpose
Than these scattered similes
I spread so full of cliché
And with no elegance at all.

And I wish to end the words
But that means ending me
And sometimes
When the words overpower my mind
That one particular thought
Doesn't seem so bad.

# Bully

Sometimes I hate
To be inside my own mind
Sitting still.
My mind enraged,
My body laid out quietly
Frantically immobile
With my head a tornado
Destroying everyone.

I feel ill but I'm not sick.
My body suffers the weight of my mind
And healthy disposition cracks
Under the strain of heavy thoughts.

I have a way with words.
I can string a line together
And dance it off my tongue.

Which means my bully has this skill too, you see.
Of course it does. It learnt it from me.

## These Pages

These pages are filled with sparse words
With too many thoughts and too many feelings.

I'm starting to think about
Beginning the process
Of giving up.

Time to get the ball rolling
From beneath this ball pit.
Time to reach up for you to hold my hand
So you can snap a picture with your phone.

What an image
Despair must create
For your deleted items
To devour.

I tried to make a stand
But then I sat back down.

I don't think I can keep
Just writing misery anymore.

So maybe I can't keep writing.

Maybe this could be my last full stop.

# A Moment's Brief Temptation

She's far away in a bed we often share
Resting under a duvet sewn together with her burdens,
Weary eyed and wearied mind,
A hundred stresses squeezed inside
A loose elastic band
Ready to snap when I return.

I'll soak up her horrors
And I'll do nothing about them but absorb,
So intense, so aggressive, so unlike you
But I'll shelter in her hostility
Because that's what I do.

She'll aim words and catch me
In her fist and squeeze fingernails to palm
Until all her burdens are bound
In my hidden sobs.

*But it's real.*

I take her pain
And I help her feel.

And then there's *you*.

A quick dream,
A beautiful lie,
Offering yourself
Though I don't know why,
A smile that doesn't kill me
And words that make me feel good
About who I am or try to be
Just like love should.
You're everyone's fantasy
And I could have you
Over her
And we'd make our Eden
And we'd never be banished
And it would be perfect.

But untrue.

See, I would rather have the misery
And take the pain as I do,
Not because it's not a fairy tale,
But because it's more real than just you.

# Busy

We're all just too busy.
You have your things
I have my things
So our things have to be on hold
For now.

It's always *for now*.

Until now lasts
Until we have lost touch
And the possibility's gone
And we can't tell one another
How busy we are anymore.

And that's how we disappear
From our lives
Despite no goodbye.

# October 1st

Today would have been the day.

It's marked in her diary in ink
And crossed out with led.

I considered calling.
My finger traced the touchscreen
And a lock screen
That used to be you
Appeared
And faded just as fast.

The home we don't share
Is empty of me
And I wonder to the point
I can't stand not knowing
If this day affects you too.

Our plans to go away
To Scotland or Cotswolds on holiday

To celebrate and say
How did we reach six years?
Feeling comfortably okay
Are there on October 1$^{st}$
With nothing
But a football fixture
Written on the lines beside it
And though there was no fight in me
I fight this day in my diary.

My tattoo has no pair
My sofa is half-seated
And my calendar is torturing me
With the reminder.

I don't miss you,
I miss what we had,
And on this day I remember
Maybe it wasn't so bad.

# Are You Enjoying Life?

✿

Are you enjoying life?
Sitting there
Caring what every
Single damn person
Thinks of you.

Is it what you imagined?
To be so concerned
By the glances of strangers
That you can't think clearly
With others
Or alone.

Is that how you wanted it?
To be so infatuated with misery
To the point that you reject
What's good for you
What's right for you
Because you're too fucking insecure
To let it be

Okay.
To just let things
Be
Okay.

*Can they ever be okay?*

Not when your self-image
Falters so much that
Your self-disgust
Is the only barrier
Between someone who finds you
So attractive
And you believing them.

It can happen
At any moment
But never a moment
If you bury your head
Deep
Deep
Deep
Into the abyss
Of your self-hatred
Self-abuse
And self-substance.

I have scars too.

They mark my arm
Beneath my tattoo.

And I hate that they are there
But they are there

And will be there whatever
So okay
They are there
And I like it
Not really
But that's how I live with it.

And you just sit there
Hating yourself so much
That you can't even function.

And your hatred is such
That the strength of it
Will never let you
Be healthy
With yourself
Or with others.

It's a decision.
The simplest and the hardest
At the same time
But a decision nonetheless.

So tell me.

Who really suffers?

Those that you push
To the corners of your life?

Or the one who you hate
To have forever
In its centre?

# How It Once Was

I used to live for the weekend
But then you were there
Always there
So when I began to crave work
I knew we were reaching
Our story's
Dead end.

I never asked for our dark,
But since the light I requested
Didn't arrive
I guess it just had to do.

I never used to say
I
At the beginning of
Every sentence
I wrote. But since
I decided
I want more

I is all
I can seem
To think about.

You're fine without me.
I'm fine alone.
We were fine together,
But it wasn't known
How fine we'd be
When we stopped
Just
Settling
For
Fine
All
The
Damn
Time.

You have to be less than fine
To be more than fine.

You have to endure the battles
To win the wars
And listen to all the clichés
Your family gives you
About better to have loved
About plenty of fish
About there's still time
About every damn word
That
Still
Means
Not

A
Damn
Thing.

I didn't want it
And neither did you.
So now we're fine apart.

And that's the only fine
That
Matters.

# I Died In My Sleep Last Night

I died in my sleep last night.
And even though my eyes opened
It was done
My mother mourned and moved on
And my effigy
Had long since finished burning.

I woke up this morning
To find the world had ended
Yet nobody knew.
People sauntered around
Unaware
That constellations of stars had exploded
Tsunamis had soaked our streets
All our hearts are bleeding
And I can't get out of bed.

I slept in your arms
And even though they weren't there
I felt them

Cold
Tightly wrapped around me
Without any comfort
At all.
They used to make my world burn
Now they barely make me simmer.

I stabbed myself to death in the night.
My hands were bloody,
I looked at what I'd done
And my alarm clock rung
And it was time to face the day.

This movement from under the covers,
Like a step from barely living
To taking the med
That makes me the walking dead.

I died in my sleep last night
And I know I'll die again today.

# In Silence

In silence we hear
What could never be spoken.
The wisdom of absence
Too loud not to learn.

There's time to whisper like it's your turn to sing,
And if you can only be one thing
- don't be brave
- don't be bold
- be silent.
Be a knowledge seeker,
Wait the few moments it takes
To start thinking deeper.
Become a seer
Like it's something you earn,
Listen to hear
Not for your talking's turn.

And when you're searching

With a broken flashlight
Stop rushing my dear –
Because in silence's wisdom
The answer you'll hear.

# I'm Sorry

You're somewhere.
I'm nowhere.
Two places that never meet.

Yet our silence is loud enough
For the whole world to hear.

I was hard to love, I know.

In the end it was too hard.

I expected nothing else.

It's time to leave once
Your good intentions runs out.

You entered with promises,
Left with anger.

I'm sorry you were the same

And I'm sorry I was to blame.

I was your world
But you were my universe.

Now we're strangers
Like we once were.
We tried not to be
But the agony of seeing you
Destroys us.

Can I be honest?

I miss you.

Relief has passed
And here we are
Or there you are
And here I am.

Alone.

Not caring.

Just as destiny beseeched me.

# Final Thoughts

Happiness is not a poetic subject
So I subject myself to misery,
As those little bites of glory
Drop and fade away
In a metaphor that did not
Quite work.

Sometimes things don't work out as planned,
Sometimes they do,
Never has something I've written
Rung so true,
So I deduce
It's a good enough excuse
To leave suicide for another day.

For now you can stand
On two glorious feet
That stood defiant in defeat
And step outside.
Prepared to meet

Prepared to mingle,
And be okay with being taken or being single
Able to look up to a world
And know as you should
That you don't need to a god to know
It is all so good.

There is meaning in nothing
There is emptiness in something
There's reason to rushing
And peace in standing still
And knowing its comforting
To be free in life
And to get your fill.

So sit up straight
Don't even wait
There's no such thing as fate
And you were meant for
More than this.

I write this again:

*You are meant for more than this.*

More than caring what who or what says,
For unteaching what you were taught,
For standing up to the bullies
That exist in your thoughts
And choosing life.

Choosing life.

I write this once more.

I.
Choose.
Life.

Hard as it my be, my dear,
Choose it with nothing to lose
And you have nothing to fear.

# I Choose

I know I've been unkind
And I know I seem resigned
To the misery I find
In this torturous incarceration of thoughts I can't get
    off my chest
And it may seem like I chose death.

And I did choose death.

For a while, I did.
And that was okay.

I seeked out the end of sorrow,
I didn't want tomorrow, want to deal,
I neglected anything that was real,
Because I dreaded that I might feel.

And that was okay.

And that is why I no longer choose death.

Because I am going to allow myself to feel it.

To feel every bit of it.
To drown myself in torture and realise
That is what life is; it's getting stuck
In the downs and the ups,
You win and you lose
And I choose...

I choose *life.*

I choose a house with the picket fence and the
    neighbours
I say hello to after picking up the kids from school
And saying things that show that I'm not cool
As I ask them about their homework
And smile at my wife
And share her Monday morning misery
And Sunday night television.

I choose the heartbreak when it all backfires
And she chooses anything but me
And my world shatters down
Because it doesn't shatter
It just shakes
And I look up and find myself in rubble;
And, yes, you can never rebuild a building exactly as
    it was—
But you can rebuild something.

I choose to rebuild.

I choose Christmases
With my family.

Watching as the toy I bought a niece or nephew
That will be next year's charity shop throw-out
Brings delight that makes the extortionate cost
Of annual consumerism
Seem like it's all just part of the magic.

I choose sad movies.
I choose to watch them with you
As we hold hands and I don't pretend not to cry
Because you, and only you, are willing to tell me
That it's okay
For a man to show he hurts when he sees pain
That brings it all back.

I choose funerals.
I choose to stand as I watch the curtain billow
In front of the coffin amidst cremation
And hear nothing but a song and some tears
But know that it's okay
As that person existed
Which was a miracle
And damn me to hell if I can't appreciate
A good miracle.

I choose my dog.
The deep yet fleeting pleasure as she needs me
And she wants to play with me
And though my arm is tired from throwing your
        toy duck
And I just want to watch television
I will throw it anyway
As there is nothing that can compare
To the sight
Of you bursting back toward me

With the duck battling the aerodynamic speed of wind
As you hold it in your mouth
And place it back on my lap.

I choose forgiveness.
For bad words and bad acts
For hurting me by shouting the facts
For cheating and abusing
Your taking and removing
And I forgive you
Not because you deserve forgiveness
But because I deserve to be free
Of all the anger
That exposes me every day.

And, most of all;
Most of all;
I choose me.
I choose to prioritise my health over your insults.
I choose to be creative and not care whether I achieve
    greatness.
I choose to make mistakes.
I choose to make lots of them.
I choose to love, freely and openly,
Like I did back when I was a teenager
And I loved for the first time
In a way that was wild
And untainted.

Yes, I think I'll choose to love.
Even though it could kill me.

And then I'll choose it again.

And again.

And again.

Because, when you take away the noise and the silence,
The fights and the defiance,
The religion and the science,
That is all you have left.

I think that will do me for now.

I think I'm quite done.

I choose love, pain, and freedom and scars.

Because, in the end,
It's all actually quite fun.

# Afterword

Thank you for reading this collection of poems about my struggle with mental health.

I hope that you have found something you can relate to, and I hope that it provides comfort in your battles.

In this afterword I am going to go explain the thoughts behind each poem. I believe that a poem should mean something different to each person that reads it, so please know that my explanations do not suggest that, if your interpretation is different to my intention, it is not valid.

If anything, that just highlights the beauty of words.

**The Struggle** is about the struggle of getting out of bed.

Some days, when the lows are at their lowest, it really does feel like you should get a medal just for getting up.

No one will ever acknowledge this battle, and nor will anyone say "well done" when they see you emerge from your bedroom after fighting the biggest battle of your day.

I go through what I need to do in my head - the turning, the swivelling, the tufts of carpet in my toes. I try to push myself out, yet I stay there.

And that is the first battle of the day, therefore it is the first battle of the book.

**Pointless Death** has the word *pointless* in its title because it is about the pointless nature of words, and how writing poem after poem about my feelings starts to feel self-indulgent.

Of course, I don't believe words are pointless. I believe they are powerful. But, sometimes, when I find myself writing another metaphor and another simile and another use of enjambment, I do wonder - is there any point to this? Am I achieving anything?

The most pertinent lines for me are "I write these words because they are harder than a blade but leave less scars." Having an outlet is a perfect alternative to self-harming, yet articulating your emotions can hurt even more. The difference is, people can't necessarily see the scars behind the words.

**Say Okay to the World** is about saying "I'm fine" when you're not.

It's okay not to be okay, yes, but people struggle to handle that. If you say you're not okay, someone may give you a pep talk or unsolicited advice or try talking you through it - then, when they are done, they expect you to be all right.

What happens when you're not still okay? When there is nothing that will make you okay? What do you say to them then?

You lie.

You say, "yeah, I'm fine," because it's the standard response and it's easier than saying "I'm really not fine."

That is what this poem is about.

**Endless Talking** was about the breakup that came before my most recent spell of misery. When you've been together for a while a breakup can take a long time - it can be discussions about problems and whether or not you should be together. This breakup was the result of talking over 2/3 months.

The only problem was that we rarely found conclusions.

There were two options - we stay together, or we don't. It seemed like neither was right, neither was wrong, they were just two options, and we had no idea which to choose.

So we talked about it to death; hence the name of the poem.

The lines "Maybe you should have stayed / Maybe I should have left" sum up the two alternatives, and neither feeling like a strong option. So I conclude, "Maybe we should have stopped the words / They mean nothing after all" - as all the incessant talking got us nowhere.

This leads onto a poem called **Okay** that I wrote a few weeks after the breakup, when my mind reluctantly mulled over the issues once again.

I'd been on a few different dates, and it felt so strange. "I just have this predisposition to fall in love with every person I kiss" highlights how vulnerable I was at the time, and how dating so soon probably wasn't the best idea. I still had a void that needed to be filled, and I would get carried away with every date just because I needed someone fill the hole that had been filled for so long.

At this point, I made the decision to stop going on dates, and to get used to being by myself before I opened myself up again.

**Fading** was about the moment where I realised I was no longer in love, months before the relationship ended.

I wanted to be in love. I really did. But I just wasn't.

I felt her "fading from my body." I wasn't angry, I was just "neutral" - it wasn't "replaced by hatred" but replaced by a "void."

And that's what started the conversation about breaking up; hence the line "Now we're in / for a conversation / more difficult / than a faulty maths equation."

The maths equation was faulty because each side wasn't balanced; just like how, in the relationship, it felt like affection was unbalanced from both sides.

The final stanza of this poem is one of my favourite stanzas I've written.

I was so afraid to break up because I didn't want the pain. I knew I'd have to go through agony to feel okay again, and I really didn't want to face it.

But it was "only temporary," and I had to remind myself of that.

And when things get bad, it feels like they just get worse and worse. That is why **They Call it Rock Bottom.**

It felt like I hit rock bottom, and I looked down, and there was all this space below rock bottom for me to keep falling.

Everyone gives you the same cliches of "it'll be all right in the end" and "what doesn't kill you makes you stronger" - but cliches are tired. When you write a cliche in a piece of writing it shows a lack of creativity, a lack of real thought as to how something actually makes you feel - but my state of mind was full of cliches.

Hence why the title includes a cliche in it.

I was running out of things to say to people, so out came the cliche.

The solution to this misery? **This Pill.**

I take a pill in the morning and a pill at night to manage my bipolar disorder. I'm pretty much fine while I'm on them, and it feels crazy that so much about my life rests upon a "1cm" pill; there is "such heavy expectation" on that pill.

And, however much the pills help, you don't just take the pills and that's that.

There are side effects.

They make me tired all the time.

And they reduce my sex drive, as shown through the line "my dick is numb." And that has always been an issue in a relationship - that I'm "tired all the time" and "I don't want to fuck."

**Inside** is one of two poems about self-harming.

I self-harmed when I was seventeen, and I ended up with scars on my arm.

But self-harm isn't just cutting. There are different levels of it.

Sometimes it can just be letting the hot tap run over your arm until you feel it hurt, and still let it run.

You want something that feels on the outside like it does on the inside.

**Graffiti** has an abrupt change of topic.

It is about the profound quotes you find in public toilets. I once saw, on the inside of a cubicle wall, the line: *War doesn't say who is right, only who is left.*

I really liked that.

Only problem was, however, this person who wrote this quote is only going to get their message across to those who are defecating.

Why not go on a march? Do something to spread your message?

A toilet wall seems like a strange place to express yourself.

**Where Are You?** is about your search for the person you are to end up with.

I write "How can I miss / Someone I don't know exists." It's strange to yearn for someone you haven't met yet.

But when you reach your thirties, and are still unmarried, and without children, I think you start to feel the ticking clock a bit more, and start to wonder if you're even capable of sustaining a relationship. To get this far without having the marriage all your friends and family have makes you wonder.

But I hope that "someday / there will no longer / be need / for these words."

Following heartbreak, there is a period of resentment, and you fade a little bit and start to feel like **I'm Not Really Here.**

I wanted to be friends with my ex, and she agreed she wanted to be friends with me. Yet I was always the one trying to stay in touch.

And I wondered whether the last person I loved would even come to my funeral.

This leads onto the second poem about self-harming, with the most common question asked when someone discovers a person's scars - **Why Did You Do That to Yourself?**

I wrote this poem with disjointed stanzas and a disjointed rhyme scheme to show the disjointed nature of your thoughts as you self-harm. To cause yourself deliberate physical pain is an extreme thing to do. Some of us are driven to it, some of us aren't - luckily, I only have memories of doing it almost 15 years ago, and have since covered the scars with a tattoo.

Back then, I had a photo frame of an ex-girlfriend that I smashed, and I used the resulting broken glass to self-harm with. This inspired the line "I smashed the photo frame and ruined her face / and the broken glass waited in place / so why not?"

I wrote **My Parent's House** about the moment you realise your parent's house is not your home anymore.

I ended up back at my parent's for a few months following this relationship as I sorted myself out - but it wasn't where I belonged anymore.

I'd grown up there. When I lived there, I'd make myself coffee every morning - but now "the coffee / it is made for me," as it is for any other guest.

It's a strange feeling when you become a guest in the home where you became an adult.

And it can make you feel a little alone, if you let it.


And I write about this, as I write about everything else, and I write and I write and I write - which leads to the poem **Yawn.**

At some point whilst writing this book it felt like I was just writing "words words words and nothing more" and that, to anyone who read it, "That's all I am."

But I have a burning need for me to put these words into my notepad.

It seemed like the only way to "end the words" would mean "ending me."

This can also be linked to the incessant thoughts of over-thinking. You analyse a situation and think and think until the words just become tired.


The next poem is about your thoughts being a **Bully.**

You can't escape your thoughts.

If a person says something nasty, you can leave the room.

A person on TV offends you, turn it off.

You can't leave your own mind.

You can "sit still" and feel "frantically immobile", as the oxymoron states.

And if I have "a way with words" so do my thoughts. I can't

control them but they have the same skills as me. They can hurt me in creative ways.

Not to be in control of your own thoughts makes you feel truly lost. It is like your mind is chaos.

And it seems like the only way to stop the thoughts is to stop writing **These Pages,** and start "to think about / beginning the process / of giving up."

I cover the pain caused post-heartbreak a few times in this anthology. That isn't to say, however, that you can't feel pain whilst in a relationship.

In **A Moment's Brief Temptation** I describe what it's like to be with someone who snaps at you because it's easy to snap at the person who's there, and you can do nothing but "shelter in her hostility." When my partner comes home angry, it seems like it's always been my role to be the punching bag.

When someone who's nice then comes along, telling you things that make you feel good about yourself, it is so tempting to throw away everything you've built for that new person.

But it's "untrue."

The one you have at home may not be the "fairytale" but they are "real." This poem is about realising it's better to have the misery with someone you love, than the temptation with someone who provides a brief way out.

Your friends become the most important thing to you when you go through a time like this. Unfortunately, when you reach out, sometimes it seems like those friends are no longer friends anymore. They have gone, without ever intending to, because you are both so **Busy.**

You promise to meet up, but you don't, and so you "disappear / from our lives / despite no goodbye."

Without those friends you can suddenly feel even more alone.

**October 1st** would have been the six year anniversary with the aforementioned girlfriend.

I came across the words written in my diary. It was a day we were planning to go away, "To Scotland or Cotswolds on holiday."

But that day is no longer an event. It's just a day. With a "football fixture" written beside it (I write all my football team's matches in my diary!)

I like the quote "It's marked in her diary in ink and crossed out in led." Ink is permanent, led can be erased. That day was still that day no matter how much either of us tried to scribble it out.

I ended up dating another woman about a month after the breakup, and we saw each other for a few weeks. It felt like it was going really well, until one day when she just had a random break down. I told her she was beautiful, and this seemed to crush her. Like she was so insecure that she couldn't handle hearing it.

She told me she cared too much about what people thought, then asked me to leave. She never spoke to me again.

And I just wondered - how can you be happy when you care so much what people think? I wanted to say to her, **Are You Enjoying Life?** How can you when you let strangers have such a hold over you?

When you care so much, the only person who suffers is you - "the one who you hate / to have forever / in its centre."

**How It Once Was** talks about how my relationship was fine. But I didn't want to settle for fine.

Was I expecting too much?

I was scared that I thought the grass would be greener, and that every relationship is just 'fine' and not spectacular.

In the end, we were fine apart, which turned out to be "the only fine that matters."

**I Died in My Sleep Last Night** talks about the feeling that you are ready to explode inside; that you are bursting with pain and anxiety - yet your outside seems so calm, so this means no one realises how much of a battle you are fighting.

When things are awful it feels like the whole world should respond as such, but the world doesn't - everything carries on.

It feels like "the world had ended / yet nobody knew."

"Constellations of stars had exploded" and "Tsunamis had soaked our streets" are things that do happen regularly, yet far away. So we carry on, as if nothing happened.

No matter how hard your pain is, life just continues.

**In Silence** is about how we talk too much, and don't realise that we need to shut up.

You can never learn while you talk.

The poem is about being quiet and just listening.

People are too busy to give advice to someone with mental health issues. They listen to respond, not to listen.

Just be quiet.

And allow the world to teach you what it needs to teach you.

**I'm Sorry** isn't an apology for heartbreak caused, but is an apology for how hard I am to deal with.

One of the toughest things about suffering from mental health issues is knowing the burden you place on those around you; knowing how your issues create anxiety for them.

I am tough to be in a relationship with. When I enter a new relationship, I'm always promised support for my issues no matter what - which is a lovely thing to say, but never turns out to be true. There is a limit to what people will take.

Now, every time I hear this declaration of support, it feels like a lie. Something they believe, but, eventually, "good intentions run out."

"I was hard to love, I know / in the end it was too hard."

Multiple relationships have ended due to my mental health making things too tough for someone who said they would stick it through.

Sometimes it feels like I have to apologise for things I can't help. Yet, if someone else said that to me about him/herself, I would tell them not to be so ridiculous.

The final two poems are, in a way, linked. **Final Thoughts** is about how writing happy poems doesn't create compelling work, so it may seem like misery is all I am preaching. But it's not. You can still "stand / on two glorious feet / that stood defiant in defeat / and step outside."

**I Choose** continues this. It seems like I've spent this book resolving myself to pain and death.

But this poem is about resolving myself to pain and life.

It is about me choosing to feel the hurt that makes us human, and see that it's not always a bad thing to feel sad.

It is about choosing life.

It is about loving freely, despite how difficult my relationship history and cynicism makes it.

It is about being brave enough to stand at a funeral and cry.

It is about prioritising my own mental health above listening to other people's comments.

There is always opportunity. There is always something for you to live for.

Sometimes you just need to change your perception.

Instead of looking at the world and thinking *I want more,* look at it and think, *isn't this amazing?*

It's a miracle to be alive, and "damn me to hell if I can't appreciate / a good miracle."

The pain conveyed in these poems isn't designed to bring you down. These words are designed to show that you are not alone. That others feel how you feel.

This final poem is designed to tell you that it is okay to feel low - and it's okay to feel high. That, despite how hard it is, you can still choose life.

It's a tough choice, and you have to make it every day, but there is always something make you choose life.

And, in the end, that is what I chose.

I choose to be happy.

And it was as easy as a choice.

Just as I choose to publish these intimate works in a little book of poetry, and entitle it, *Mental Health and Me.*

## Sign up for One Poem a Week

For your free poems visit
www.lifeinwordspoetry.com/sign-up

Also Available

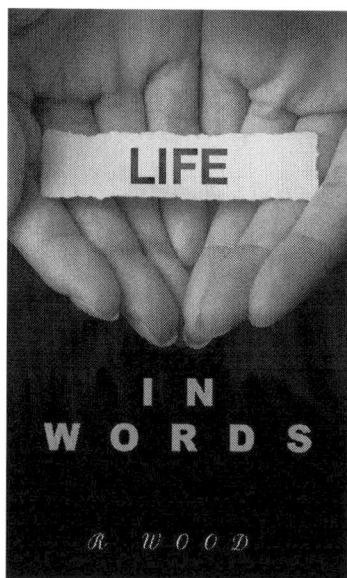

Printed in Great Britain
by Amazon